Baby animal names

Bobbie Kalman

 Crabtree Publishing Company

www.crabtreebooks.com

Created by Bobbie Kalman

Author and Editor-in-Chief
Bobbie Kalman

Educational consultants
Reagan Miller
Elaine Hurst
Joan King

Editors
Joan King
Reagan Miller
Kathy Middleton

Proofreader
Crystal Sikkens

Design
Bobbie Kalman
Katherine Berti

Photo research
Bobbie Kalman

Production coordinator
Katherine Berti

Prepress technician
Katherine Berti

Photographs
BigStockPhoto: p. 10
Other photographs by Shutterstock

Library and Archives Canada Cataloguing in Publication

Kalman, Bobbie, 1947-
  Baby animal names / Bobbie Kalman.

(My world)
ISBN 978-0-7787-9421-9 (bound).--ISBN 978-0-7787-9465-3 (pbk.)

    1. Animals--Infancy--Juvenile literature.
I. Title. II. Series: My world (St. Catharines, Ont.).

QL763.K34 2010   j591.3'9   C2009-906056-6

Library of Congress Cataloging-in-Publication Data

Kalman, Bobbie.
  Baby animal names / Bobbie Kalman.
    p. cm. -- (My world)
  ISBN 978-0-7787-9465-3 (pbk. : alk. paper) -- ISBN 978-0-7787-9421-9
(reinforced library binding : alk. paper)
  1. Animals--Infancy--Juvenile literature. I. Title. II. Series.

QL763.K355 2010
591.3'9--dc22
                                                    2009040958

Crabtree Publishing Company

Printed in China/122009/CT20091009

www.crabtreebooks.com   1-800-387-7650

Published in Canada
Crabtree Publishing
616 Welland Ave.
St. Catharines, Ontario
L2M 5V6

Published in the United States
Crabtree Publishing
PMB 59051
350 Fifth Avenue, 59th Floor
New York, New York 10118

Published in the United Kingdom
Crabtree Publishing
Maritime House
Basin Road North, Hove
BN41 1WR

Published in Australia
Crabtree Publishing
386 Mt. Alexander Rd.
Ascot Vale (Melbourne)
VIC 3032

Words to know

pouch

bear
cub

fox kit
or pup

goat
kid

kangaroo
joey

koala
joey

raccoon
kittens

wolf
cub

Children are called **kids**.

Baby **goats** are called kids, too.

Baby **cats** are called **kittens**.

Did you know that baby **raccoons** are called kittens, too?

A baby **dog** is called a **puppy**.

Did you know that a baby **fox** is called a **pup** or a **kit**?

Did you know that a baby **wolf**
is called a pup or a **cub**?

Did you know that a baby **bear** is also called a cub?

A baby **kangaroo** is called a **joey**.
The joey lives in its mother's **pouch**.

pouch

Did you know that a baby **koala** is called a joey, too? The baby koala also lives in its mother's pouch.

Activity

How many baby animal names do you know?

A baby horse is called a **foal**.

A baby rabbit is called a **bunny**.

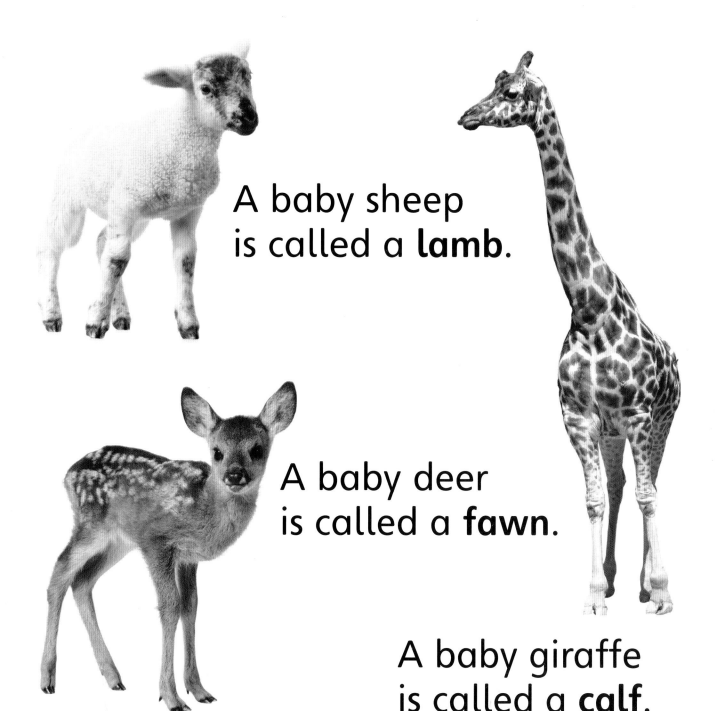

A baby sheep
is called a **lamb**.

A baby deer
is called a **fawn**.

A baby giraffe
is called a **calf**.

15

Notes for adults

What's in a name?

Baby animal names helps children learn the names of animals and what they are called as babies. Ask the children if they think baby goats are like children and if raccoons are like cats, since they share the same baby names. Make a list of all the nicknames the children were called when they were babies.

Animal match-ups

Create an animal match-up game to help reinforce new animal vocabulary and place memory. Create a set of cards with pictures showing the baby animals in the book. On a separate set of cards, write the name of the baby animal (kit, joey, cub, foal, calf). Lay out the cards face down on the floor. Ask the students to take turns turning over two cards to make as many matches as they can.

It's Fun to Learn about Baby Animals Series contains wonderful books about baby animals that introduce children to animal families, species, life cycles, and many more concepts.
Guided Reading: J

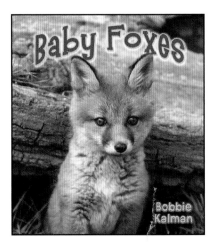